Well written, makes you think and definitely worth a read! Thought provoking!
So many distinctly chosen words that trigger past, present and future thoughts and emotions! Really enjoyed reading! Definitely a well written collection of poems and worth the time! A very talented author!—BRB

******

An Enjoyable and Humorous Collection of Poetry!
An enjoyable collection of entertaining poems written by a talented poet. Richard Buchanan has an innate ability to take everyday subjects and creative a clever rhyming poem out of them. He has a fun and comedic sense of humor and expert timing that he disperses throughout his poetry making for an enjoyable read. I copy edited his work and thoroughly enjoyed it. I found myself chuckling over some of his humorous poems and feeling the angst and sadness of others. One of my favorite poems is about his grandson, Max. It touched my heart with its tenderness. I have worked with Richard on previous books and enjoyed working with him again on this book. I highly recommend this fine collection which is interspersed with readers' comments and quotes from famous and not so famous people.—Jjspina

******

Very enjoyable, a great read and very entertaining.
I've enjoyed poetry since I was a small child and would listen with rapt attention as my great aunt would read to me at bedtime—always some form of rhyming poetry. I bought this book on a whim and I am so glad that I did. It's delightful and made me laugh at some of the poems and cry at others. I think all of these poems will give the reader pause for thought and will touch their hearts in an unexpected and joyful way. A nice escape, if only temporarily, from the woes and problems of our world today.—SKE

******

Witty, humorous, universal life subjects.
Witty, humorous, straightforward rhyme. For someone like me, who often does not understand poetry, this is perfect. Especially liked the many quotes following each poem relating to it's subject matter, some debatable, however. The author provides the personal genesis to each of his poems. Not much metaphorical imagery, just straightforward life situational ink, much of which is biographically inspired!—Gitfish

Don't miss this poetry book!
You will really enjoy reading this poetry book. It is like no other I've seen. I love the subject matter as many poems deal with real life and the intros before each poem help you to understand the thoughts, humor and emotion that went into each poem. I also love the quotes from famous people. I promise you'll enjoy it!—VB

******

Personal Stories that are witty.
This book of poetry was creative, witty and real. Has several personal stories that makes you feel connected to the writer.—Rachel Wunch

******

This is a delightful book!
I thoroughly enjoyed this poetry—I keep the book on my coffee table-friends see it asked about it—start to read through and become captured. The poems address so many real life situations—physical and emotion—his book is almost a text for life.—LAF

******

A fun read
What an enjoyable read! The author is so witty, real and writes with grace. I think I will go get a Krispy Kreme donut and repeat my journey through this awesome poetry book!—Jwh

"I will be generous with my love today. I will sprinkle compliments and uplifting words everywhere I go. I will do this knowing that my words are like seeds and when they fall on fertile soil, a reflection of those seeds will grow into something greater."

Steve Maraboli, Life, the Truth, and Being Free

"Feel compliments as deeply as you feel insults."

James Clear

Symmetry in Poetry

Rhyming poetry can be fun, especially, correctly done…

By Richard Buchanan

"You want to know how to rhyme, then learn how to add. It's mathematics."

Mos Def

"Making words rhyme for a living is one of the great joys of my life. That's a superpower I've been very conscious of developing. I started at the same level as everybody else, and then I just listened to more music and talked to myself until it was an actual superpower I could pull out on special occasions."

Lin-Manuel Miranda

"To me, a poem that's in rhyme and meter is the difference between watching a film in full color and watching a film in black and white. Not that a few black and white films aren't wonderful. So are certain successful pieces of free verse."

X. J. Kennedy

"Painting is silent poetry, and poetry is painting that speaks."

Plutarch

"Every heart sings a song, incomplete, until another heart whispers back. Those who wish to sing always find a song. At the touch of a lover, everyone becomes a poet."

Plato

Published by Kindle Direct Publishing
Cover design by Richard Buchanan

Copy Editor: Janice Spina, Jemsbooks; http://jemsbooks.com
Multi-award-winning author:
Pinnacle Book Achievement Awards
Reader's Favorite Award Winner - Silver Medal & Honorable Mention
Authors Cover Contest - Silver Medal
Mom's Choice Awards - Silver Medal

Forth Edition: April 2022

ISBN: 9781095558317

"Certainly the interest in asserting copyright is a justified one."

Johannes Rau

"The right to be attributed as an author of a work is not merely a copyright, it is every author's basic human right."

Kalyan C. Kankanala

Contents

"If you would not be forgotten, As soon as you are dead and rotten, Either write things worth reading, Or do things worth the writing."

Benjamin Franklin

"Poetry is when an emotion has found its thought and the thought has found words."

Robert Frost

Contents Continued

"I love words—I don't like strange ones. You don't understand 'em and they don't understand you. Old words are like old friends, you know 'em the minute you see 'em."

Will Rogers

"Pure mathematics is, in its way, the poetry of logical ideas."

Albert Einstein

<u>**Dedication**</u>

This book is dedicated to a caring and very helpful former colleague.

John W. Howell, author of thriller, fiction books **The Contract**, **Circumstances of Childhood**, **My Girl**, **His Revenge**, and **Our Justice**, is a novelist and businessman that I have respected since the day I initially met him.

My first encounter with John was decades ago, when as a young man, I joined a company where as it turned out, John was working at a very fitting and important managerial position. I worked under his skillful leadership for many, many years. And during that time, I learned a lot from John about running a profitable business, creating a management team that delivers on its promises, and developing team leadership skills.

Not long after I retired, I began writing rhyming poetry. And realizing that by that time, John had achieved a well-deserved and respected status among successful thriller novelists, I reached out to him for some advice and guidance in my quest to become a valued writer of rhyming poetry.

If it weren't for John's selfless instructs, I would not be a part of the poetry scene today. Thanks John!

"When you have wit of your own, it's a pleasure to credit other people for theirs."

Criss Jami

"Develop an attitude of gratitude, and give thanks for everything that happens to you, knowing that every step forward is a step toward achieving something bigger and better than your current situation."

Brian Tracy

"No duty is more urgent than that of returning thanks."

James Allen

About the Author

Richard Buchanan has 37 years of experience in the consumer products industry, working in various sales and marketing capacities, undertaking increasing domestic and international responsibilities, with much success in all positions.

Richard retired in 2005 at the age of 56, in order to pursue his interests in writing poetry, physical fitness, reading, cruising the Caribbean, trading equity options, and drumming. He lives in Plano, Texas and has been a proud Texan for over 35 years.

Author's Notes

Rhyming poetry done well, can be very pleasing to the ear, and fun to read. And when the poetry tells a story one can relate to in some way, then the poet has succeeded in communicating with his reader.

I painstakingly create my poetry using true-rhymes, consistent rhyming and syllabic conventions, and uniform accents. Each and every poem I've included in this book has a rhythmic cadence to it, which hopefully makes it more enjoyable for one to read.

I have written an introduction to most of my poems, revealing why I wrote the poem, the inspiration behind the poem, and some context to aid the reader in unpacking as much meaning as possible from every line of my poetry.

And finally, I've included some complimentary feedback from a few of my poetry colleagues, as well as some applicable quotes by famous and not so famous personalities, in the hopes that the comments and quotes will add pleasure to your reading experience. I have tried to make this book as entertaining as possible.

"All good books are alike in that they are truer than if they had really happened. And after you are finished reading one, you will feel that all that happened to you and afterwards, it all belongs to you: the good and the bad, the ecstasy, the remorse and sorrow, the people and the places, and how the weather was. If you can get so that you can give that to people, then you are a writer."

Ernest Hemingway

1. "Writing Rhyming Poetry"

Most folks don't realize the additional challenges involved in writing rhyming poetry versus writing free-verse poetry. Writing free-verse poetry permits poets all the leeway they desire in order to explore the inspirational depths of their vivid imaginations without any restraints. The authors of rhyming poetry however, do not have that same generous poetic latitude.

Rhyming poetry requires the poet to follow strict syllabic conventions, true rhyming patterns, and consistent accent rules; all the while telling an interesting story to which readers easily relate. And most importantly, a rhythmic, easy cadence.

I admire free-verse poets. However, I have always had a bent towards math, problem solving, symmetry and the like. So it seems very natural for me to write rhyming poetry, even with all the very strict protocols to which I must adhere. Variations of some of the conventions I've used to create my poetry can be found on page 81.

I sincerely hope that you'll enjoy my poems, be they happy, sad, funny, or heartfelt.

The following poem, *Writing Rhyming Poetry,* won the Second Place Silver Award in a recent AllPoetry contest. AllPoetry is recognized as the largest on-line poetry group in the USA, and posts thousands of poems from poets all over the world.

Poetry that rhymes is fun,
Especially, correctly done.
But it's not easy; no it's not.
It takes much work, and lots of thought.

What's the first thing you must do?
There's several things—I'll name a few.
Intriguing story; real true rhymes,
And that, I'll say a hundred times.

Accents, they're important too.
You'll need a cadence through and through.
Add syllable consistency,
And you've got rhyming poetry.

"Imagination was given to man to compensate him for what he is not, and a sense of humor was provided to console him for what he is."

Oscar Wilde

"My mother was always fascinated with the fact that I could rhyme so much stuff."

Dolly Parton

"I love rhymes; I love to write a poem about New York and rhyme oysters with The Cloisters. And The lady from Knoxville who bought her brassieres by the boxful. I just feel a sort of small triumph."

Garrison Keillor

"Some people imagine that rhyme interferes with the rational processes of thought by obliging us to distort what we originally had in mind. But are rational processes so important? In many of us, even in poets, they can be dull and predictable. An interruption, a few detours and unexpected turns, might make a trip with them less routine. The necessity of finding a rhyme may jolt the mind out of its ruts, force it to turn wildly across the fields in some more exhilarating direction. Force it out of the world of reason into the world of mystery, magic, and imagination, in which relationships between sounds may be as exciting as a great idea."

John Frederick Nims and David Mason

"Writing poetry is a passion, ignited by thoughts, fueled by ink. A way to travel through another mind, where souvenirs of tears are tucked away inside your soul. Or leave you with smiles for miles, depending on which route you go."

Renee Dixon

Hiker1 - *Thank you for this lovely poem. Fun, light and simple. Nicely done sir.*

2. "Tides of My Heart"

For decades now, I've vacationed at the South Jersey Shore. From the time I was a little boy, I've been mesmerized by the actions of the waves and tides. The force of the gravitational pull of the ocean's tides, sometimes serves to explain why two people can be so strongly attracted to each other. I hope you enjoy this love poem.

Watching the ocean, just pounding the shore.
Same steady movement; same punch as before.
Vigorous motion; it's all on display.
Twenty-four hours of every long day.

From the beginning, the waves nature makes,
Always keep rolling, not pausing for breaks.
What makes those waves grow, then topple and crash?
Calm seas or bad storms, they build, then they bash.

Scientists tell us the moon is the cause;
Oceans responding to gravity's laws.
That's how the tides work; first high tide, then low.
Moon forcing oceans first to, and then fro.

Vast shifting oceans prove forces untold.
One can't deny it, the ocean's controlled.
Your gaze has forces of gravity too.
Having the power that triple moons do.

Tides of my heart girl are pulling on me.
Pulling me toward you degree by degree.
Something about you that sets you apart.
I can't explain it, you pull on my heart.

Offered three wishes, I'd need only one.
One wish for you dear and then I'd be done.
You are the one love I've longed to soon find.
Come to me darling, leave all else behind.

"You know you're in love when you can't fall asleep because reality is finally better than your dreams."

Dr. Seuss

"I love you so much my heart is sure. As time goes on I love you more, your happy smile, your loving face, no one will ever take your place."

Unknown

"I could not tell if I loved you the first moment I saw you, or if it was the second, third or fourth. But I remember the first moment I looked at you walking toward me and realized that somehow the rest of the world seemed to vanish when I was with you."

Cassandra Clare

"If you fall in a river, There is a Boat, If you fall in a well, There is a Rope, But if you fall in Love, There is no Hope."

Unknown

"It's a blessed thing to love and feel loved in return."

E.A. Bucchianeri, Brushstrokes of a Gadfly

Man - *This was pretty awesome. The way everything went together was great and well-coordinated.*

Poetblue13 - *I loved the easy flow of this poem and how from the opening line, we are drawn into the body of the write effortlessly. The descriptive work here is light and relevant and the writer's intent is never in doubt. This ends on a hopeful note which completes the 'happiness' factor this poem delivers. Very nice work. Lovely.*

Davidcooler889 - *Wow, a beautiful, perfect poem. You're a great writer, I'll tell you that!*

3. "On-Line Dating"

Finding myself single as a senior, and not particularly wanting to spend the remainder of my life without loving a woman or feeling the love of a wonderful woman, I investigated, and subsequently joined, an on-line dating service that seemed age-appropriate for my stage of life.

There is a certain calmness that comes from the simplicity of being single and living alone, that was soon challenged within the first few contacts I received from female subscribers to the same dating site. I had spent a good deal of my time on-line answering the dating site's questions about me, my wants, my needs, my likes, and my dislikes, presumably so that the dating service could send so called *perfect* matches my way. So, why would I be getting *winks* and *flirts* from women eight states away, having completely different profiles than the *looking-for* profile I had initially spelled out in detail for the dating service?

As time went on, I experienced a couple of dates with women who hardly said a word. Some women I met, were building a bullpen of men; a stable if you will. And then they would schedule each of their men on a well thought-out dating rotation— free dinner after free dinner after free dinner, never intending to narrow down the field to one special guy. Every once in a while, I would meet a woman who would turn out to be a workaholic and have no time at all to date. Odd that she would be on a dating site in the first place. What an experience!

Awkward is dating, as one's getting older.
Seeking and searching; first warmer, then colder.
Countless attempts of soon finding a dream-date;
Finding a truelove, and finding a soul-mate.

Looking through screen glare, a *flirt*—it's a breakthrough!
Then, out of nowhere, *I'd like to soon meet you.*
Feeling my heart stir, she's got my attention;
Sounding distinctive in every dimension.

Seems like she's feisty, and cute, smart, beguiling,
In'tresting, happy, and constantly smiling.
Sometimes I wonder, if I'm merely dreaming.
Why since her *flirt* came, has my face been beaming?

Nervously waiting to finally meet her.
Angst not abating, I'm starting to teeter.
Seeing her coming, I start to get heady.
God, what an angel, I love her already.

Gladly, I'll tell you, our luncheon was splendid.
She and I both knew, of what we intended.
Dating for months now, she's all I can think of.
Managing somehow, we both found our truelove.

"Love is an irresistible desire to be irresistibly desired."

Robert Frost

"Patience is a virtue and the best things in life are worth waiting for."

Julie Spira

"In all the world, there is no heart for me like yours. In all the world, there is no love for you like mine."

Maya Angelou

"A soul-mate is someone who has locks that fit our keys, and keys to fit our locks. When we feel safe enough to open the locks, our truest selves step out and we can be completely and honestly who we are; we can be loved for who we are and not for who we're pretending to be. Each unveils the best part of the other. No matter what goes wrong around us, with that one person we're safe in our own paradise."

Richard Bach

Johnrm23 -*This is nicely written, I enjoyed the read and I truly do hope you find truelove.*

4. "Caution"

St. Thomas, in the U.S. Virgin Islands, is well-known for its legendary history of pirates, sugar cane plantations, and even cannibals. But nowadays, it's known for its beaches, snorkeling, and tourism. Located some 1,100 miles southeast of Miami, St. Thomas consists of seaside cliffs, mountains with lush forests up to 1,500 feet high, and miles and miles of pristine, white, sandy beaches.

My wife and I visited St. Thomas a few years back, and promptly rented a jeep in order to explore the island and experience its stunning vistas. The challenging, winding mountain roads were steep, narrow, and in a lot of cases, in need of some serious repair. But the sights were breathtaking, once we arrived at the peak—well worth the tedious drive.

Along the way, I was amused to notice the many roadside advertisements, paid for by a particular topless bar over in Red Hook. There were dozens of them. Almost at every stop sign or traffic light, I'd see another placard asking one-and-all to come to the club for *sights* of a different kind.

At one point, while stoped at a mountain-side red light, I was staring at yet another one of those topless bar invitations, and I began daydreaming about writing a poem describing these colorful depictions of an absolutely beautiful, half-naked woman, when all-of-a-sudden, a loud horn from another jeep behind us, and a sharp elbow to my ribs from my wife, brought me back down to earth. Busted!

The islands? They're Virgin.
But Flo? Not so much.
Her road signs invite you,
To look, but don't touch.

Her picture's enticing,
But stare not too long.
You'll not see the green light,
Or make your turn wrong.

There's one other warning,
You'll need to abide.
If wife sees you staring,
There's nowhere to hide.

"A strip club is one of the few places where two groups voluntarily come together who have such precipitous contrasts in net worth and familiarity with violence, each group with a head-and-shoulders edge in one category. The basic math of a tropical storm."

Tim Dorsey, Florida Roadkill

"He offered her the world. She said she had her own."

Anonymous

"I understood and agreed that from a feminist perspective working in a strip club was extremely problematic, but I was saving money to travel, and making more in one night than most of my friends made in a week. Plus, it was interesting."

Periel Aschenbrand

"I really like the Caribbean. Anyplace in the Caribbean. I get there, and I feel like a monkey—the perfect state."

Penelope Cruz

"Visual surprise is natural in the Caribbean; it comes with the landscape, and faced with its beauty, the sigh of history dissolves."

Derek Walcott

T Ashok - *Very cute. Lovely. Loved the If wife sees you staring.... Brought a big smile.*

Hosein shafiei - *Lovely poem....very good imagery .....well penned....keep writing.*

5. "Failure"

Failure can cause us to feel helpless, but it can also bring hope, while it pushes us to refocus on making wise choices. You have the power to take control of your destiny.

Failure kills one's motivation.
Sadly, that's a fact of life.
It does its best to mess us up:
It quells our dreams, it wreaks its strife.

Failure's absolute in mortals;
Makes one feel like they're unfit.
Discouragement is failure's curse:
Throw-in that towel, despair, then quit.

I've known failure all my life and
Many times I've felt it's sting.
I've tried real hard to overcome.
But frankly, I've not learned a thing.

What on earth are we to do then,
If in fact it's preordained?
And how should mankind now proceed?
And what have experts ascertained?

Hamstrung by our pains of failure,
Some say, may provoke success,
Provide a pathway to our goals,
Renew our purpose, ease our stress.

Famous and successful folks have
Stumbled and become distraught.
But what they really want then, is
A chance to take another shot.

Be of courage, seek your strength and
Claim exceptionality.
Do not forget that you're in charge
And you control your destiny.

6. "The State of Brick and Mortar Retail"

We've all been there; we've all experienced this. Whether we're walking through a large Grocery Store, looking for something in a giant Home Improvement Center, or searching through a big Box Store; *where are all the employees?* And furthermore, where is the manager, when the store has one checker line open, and way too many folks waiting to be checked out? I don't understand why it's so difficult to get help.

Focused—striding purposely,
Throughout a great big giant store.
Searching, hunting for a clue
To where is, what I'm looking for.

Worn out from my fruitless schlep;
Just, how long should I persevere?
Hoping I would find some help
And quickly get-on-outa-here.

Spotting three employees grouped:
As in a conversation pit.
Two that couldn't care much less,
And one that didn't give a shit.

Leaving now with empty arms,
I met a man; the boss, his guise.
Asking: *Did you find it all?*
I peered into his vacant eyes.

Totally devoid of goods,
I clearly did not *find it all*!
Surely he must have a brain;
The question is: How very small?

Getting home remembering,
The apathy I'd come upon,
Booting up my good ole Dell,
I clicked on trusted Amazon.

"Spend a lot of time talking to customers face to face. You'd be amazed how many companies don't listen to their customers."

Ross Perot

"Your most unhappy customers are your greatest source of learning."

Bill Gates

"The goal as a company is to have customer service that is not just the best but legendary."

Sam Walton

"Make your product easier to buy than your competition, or you will find your customers buying from them, not you."

Mark Cuban

"Your customer doesn't care how much you know until they know how much you care."

Damon Richards

"Customers don't expect you to be perfect. They do expect you to fix things when they go wrong."

Donald Porter

"He profits most who serves best."

Arthur F. Sheldon

7. "Second Marriages"

My first marriage lasted over 20 years and produced two of the most gifted and talented children ever brought into this world by a husband and a wife. But maybe I'm biased. Unfortunately, circumstances beyond our control weakened our marriage, and without the skill set necessary to navigate through the hard times, we divorced. I'm pleased and proud to say however, that we are very good friends to this day.

After a season of being single, I married once again. My own children were grown, but my second wife had two teenage girls. They were both very accepting, supportive, and loving from the time our courtship began, until the day we divorced, some 16 years later. Then, they disavowed my existence, and worse, cut me off from seeing my four grandkids.

I think, while step-children seem to be similar to biological children, the reality is, the two are as different as night and day. There will never be a love commitment fused by blood and history between a step-dad and his step-children.

Since I've been married twice and divorced twice, I've done quite a lot of soul searching as to how and why these second marriages are so inclined to fail. I've researched the subject on the internet and I've discussed this topic with many twice divorced men. The conclusion I've drawn is, that by the time two people decide to get married for a second time, they are completely set in their own ways. They are already surrounded by a network of friends, and usually, the top spot in their life is not really vacant or available—that special spot has already been taken by a grandchild, a dog, a horse, a hobby, or unfortunately one's own narcissism. So, the highest spot a potential second marriage spouse can hope for is second place, and sadly, many times much farther down the pecking order. So, my point is this. If you're considering getting married for a second time, please make sure you are capable and willing to put your potential spouse on a pedestal as the number one person in your life. But if your potential spouse isn't willing to do the same, it might be better not to get involved in Second Marriages.

> A stepdad who thinks he's the real dad's a fool.
> He thinks he's so righteous, so noble, so cool.
> But if truth were known,
> Wife's kids become grown,
> Their patronization is rife, as a rule.

The bride and the groom just assume it will work.
They never consider what issues might lurk.
Their heads in the sand,
Their future unplanned,
They rush into marriage; good judgment they shirk.

The second of marriages, patently tough,
When problems arise, spouses sharply rebuff.
It's grueling to talk,
Too easy to walk,
So being in love is not nearly enough.

The reason that couples like this can't survive;
Their deep down priorities, sadly don't jive.
If he hangs her moon,
While she makes him swoon,
And all else comes second—relationships thrive.

"To love and be loved is to feel the sun from both sides."

David Viscott

"Maybe the difference between first marriage and second marriage is that the second time at least you know you are gambling."

Elizabeth Gilbert

"A bride at her second marriage does not wear a veil. She wants to see what she is getting."

Hellen Rowland

"Marriage is the triumph of imagination over intelligence. Second marriage is the triumph of hope over experience."

Oscar Wilde

"I have learned that only two things are necessary to keep one's wife happy. First, let her think she's having her own way. And second, let her have it."

Lyndon B. Johnson

"As somebody who, in my second marriage, insisted on a prenuptial agreement, I can also testify that sometimes it is an act of love to chart the exit strategy before you enter the union, in order to make sure that not only you, but your partner as well, knows that there will be no World War III should hearts and minds, for any sad reason, change."

Elizabeth Gilbert

"I picked my first husband, God picked my second husband."

Charlie Price

Archie20 - *AWESOME...Great share...Beautiful piece....very finely written from Heart & Soul...I'm blessed to read....Honestly I loved it & great salute...AMAZING...Keep going...INSPIRED...God bless!*

Jan Serene - *Marriage in itself without offspring is hard enough. In the beginning, our hearts and minds are floating on a cloud until the reality of everyday living hits us like a lead balloon. I don't have children but I've been married twice and I'm still married. I believe the key to any relationship is understanding the other, not necessarily agreeing with everything but being able to communicate your feelings void of defensive words or actions.*

Poetconception - *What you have offered the world should be emblazoned in large bold letters. It is so true that it hurts. Went through something similar although the second didn't last but my third one is going on 27 years and her kids think I'm an okay guy. Thanks for sharing this, sometimes, unfortunate truth. Inspiring.*

the.amateur.poet - *Wow, it is so nicely written and really captures the point you were making.*

SnehaWassan - *Strong powerful write. Very Nicely portrayed. Keep writing!*

8. "Regret Hangs on Where Opportunity Once Existed"

I'll bet that many if not all of us, have thought about regrets in our lives from time to time; those opportunities that have passed us by for various self-inflicted reasons. Wondering what could have been, if only we had taken advantage of those opportunities, can haunt us for the rest of our lives—or not. This poem was voted among many, to be published by The Society of Classical Poets. I was honored to be chosen and published by such a respected literary giant. I hope you all enjoy this heart-felt poem.

There are lots of sad words we lament with such ease,
But there's none any sadder and mournful than these:
I regret my decisions, and wish to go back
To that Y in the road where my life went off track.

I was foolhardy, reckless, and to my dismay,
I embarked on a road I regret to this day.
During high school I wish I had not been so bored.
I excelled playing sports, but the books I ignored.

Then in college, I realized I wasn't prepared.
And in no time at all, *you've flunked out,* they declared.
I reluctantly started to find my own way,
But without any skills, drifted farther astray.

My self-image: a laggard who's filled with self-blame.
Till a therapist said, *with mistakes, there's no shame.*
So I tried to forgive myself—set myself free.
And to focus on being the best I could be.

It took time and hard work and my progress was slow,
But I stuck to my plan and soon started to grow.
My esteem soon improved like my therapist said,
I was drifting no more—started winning instead.

It's amazing how winning's transforming my soul.
Gaining confidence now, I can reach any goal.
My regrets still hang on, but they own me no more;
I'm not haunted by *what could've been,* like before.

"We crucify ourselves between two thieves—regret for the past and fear of the future."

Fulton Oursler

"Life's too short, time's too precious, and stakes too high to dwell on what might have been."

Hilary Clinton

"Regret of neglected opportunity is the worst hell that a living soul can inhabit."

Rafael Sabatini

"Regret is an appalling waste of energy, you can't build on it—it's only good for wallowing in."

UnKnown

"We have to let go of all blame, all attacking, all judging, to free our inner selves to attract what we say we want."

Joe Vital

"We should regret our mistakes and learn from them, but never carry them forward into the future with us."

Lucy Maud Montgomery

"A man is not old until regrets take the place of dreams."

John Barrymore

"It's human nature to want to go back and fix things or change things that we regret."

John Gray

Thwarted777 - *"My regrets still exist but they own me no more." That's the best way to look at our past. Remarkable writing of a slandered past that turned a corner of understanding and confidence. Thank you for sharing!*

9. Six Silly Little Limericks

The Russians at last did their deed.
They warned us but we did not heed.
'Twas good for the masses!
According to asses:
Obama, Pelosi, and Reed.

A large English family named Kratz,
Lived crowded in two run-down flats.
They wanted to move,
But first they must prove,
No co-habitation with rats.

There once was a cold day in Hell,
That broke a hot blistering spell.
Caused pigs to take flight,
And day to turn night,
Said Facebook and Twitter as well.

Distinguished was Doctor James Felch.
But dining, he'd frequently belch.
Guests said that was rude,
Some even said crude,
But belching he never did squelch.

'Twas out of my sight and my mind,
If blind did indeed lead the blind.
But snoozing and loosing,
And cruising for bruising
Sound trite and at best unrefined.

Our doctors we like 'cause we know.
But under the Care Act they'll go.
So when coverage ends,
We'll go to our friends,
For prostate exams quid-pro-quo.

10. "Our Dear Savanah"

Recently, I was asked to write a poem celebrating one particular family; a daughter graduating from high school, soon to leave home for a brand new adventure at college, and her parents who couldn't have been more proud of her. Her loving grandmother requested that I recite it at her granddaughter's graduation party.

Richard and Angie, now blessedly wed.
No dream out-of-reach, as cloud nine lay ahead.
Smart and hard-working, employment secured.
Embarked on a quest, bliss all but assured.

Friendship, devotion, and love filled their hearts.
A love that matured; yes indeed, off the charts.
Living the good life, success now attained.
Yet starting to think, there's more to be gained.

Pondering children; their dogs once sufficed,
They soon longed to bear a sweet child to love Christ.
Pregnant with baby, fulfilling God's plans,
A marvelous girl, God formed in His hands.

Baby turned child now, continued to grow.
Angelic and strong, and her halo aglow.
High school so easy, the time just slipped by.
Always excelling, and then came good-bye.

Friendly, kind, loving, compassionate too,
And in a few months, she begins life anew.
Family and friends here, pray wisdom and health;
A wonderful life, and plenty of wealth.

"Do not go where the path may lead; go instead where there is no path and leave a trail."

Ralph Waldo Emerson

11. "Tribute to Shake Shack"

I had never set foot in a Shake Shack Restaurant until one recently opened right around the corner from where I live. I had no idea what to expect upon joining the queue in front of the store, but I immediately knew that something very exciting was going on, because there were about 30 other people waiting in line to get in.

My experience was like no other casual dining experience I've ever had. Not only was the food outrageously delicious, but it was extremely healthy as well. And the customer service was so relaxed, friendly, and caring, they made me feel like I was family.

When I got home, I decided to do a little research on this newfound gem of a restaurant. I learned that a man by the name of Danny Meyer was behind the original concept and the initial stand and store in Manhattan. Another man, Randy Garutti has been responsible for the chain's successful growth throughout subsequent years. Their simple mantras from the beginning have always been: *Quality Ingredients and Extraordinary Service,* and *Stand for Something Good.*

I was most impressed with the very simple, but non-negotiable principles that have been marinated into every employee on the team. For instance, Shake Shack only sources high-quality natural ingredients, they cook all of their food to order, and they place a major emphasis on the happiness and contentment of their employees and customers.

Long ago, Mr. Meyer created a set of priorities which encompass his philosophy of *Enlightened Hospitality*. Simply stated, the idea was to create a calm, *welcoming atmosphere* for everyone involved with Shake Shack; the customers, employees, suppliers, everyone. Over the years he has perfected a style of *relaxed, but highly polished service*.

Mr. Garutti makes an effort to empower his employees to do whatever it takes to make his customers feel loved. He's even coined the phrase, *Radical Hospitality*. At one of his pep talks to the staff of a new store at its grand opening, in order to drive home the idea of *Radical Hospitality*, he challenged the group: *If there's a kid crying, who's going to walk over with a free cup of custard?* He continually tells new employees, *be excellent, be genuine, be friendly and eager and human.*

Sitting in Shake Shack, long wait now behind.
Soaking the vibes in, Fast-Food redefined.
Smi'ling and happy, now thinking 'bout food,
Feeling quite special; much better's my mood.

Excellent service from nice, friendly pros,
Proved I was right 'bout the rest'rant I chose.
Hearing kids crying, I turn and I see,
Loving and caring; a custard for free.

Founded way back in two thousand and one;
Hot dog with mustard, a smile, and a bun.
Moved from a cart in two thousand and four.
Permanent space now, from kiosk to store.

Humble beginnings to stores 'round the land,
Shake Shack's become now, a world renowned brand.
Fine casual dining in welcoming stores,
Brings in those patrons who flood through their doors.

Standing for something worthwhile, as they stood,
Not for just something, but something that's good.
Only the highest of quality served;
All-nat'ral, healthy—high standards preserved.

Serving fresh burgers, and hot dogs, and fries,
Soft serve, and chicken, and milk shakes—their prize.
Fresh natural Angus, no hormones allowed.
Antibiotics were banned, they've avowed.

Customer service, just way off the charts,
Links their great name to their customer's hearts.
Trained and enlightened, hospitable too,
Staff here excels while they strive to out-do.

Kevin's in charge of the Shake Shack next door.
Truly he runs it like it's his own store.
Friendly, hard-working, he's so full of zest,
That's why his Shake Shack is clearly the best.

"Success in business requires training, discipline and hard work. If you're not frightened by these things, the opportunities are just as great today as they ever were."

David Rockefeller

"Things that you are unlikely to regret: exercise, eating healthily, challenging yourself, making a plan, being kind."

Freequill

"A great restaurant doesn't distinguish itself by how few mistakes it makes but by how well they handle those mistakes."

Danny Meyer, Shake Shack *"A great restaurant is one that just makes you feel like you're not sure whether you went out or you came home, and confuses you. If it can do both of those things at the same time, you're hooked."*

Danny Meyer, Shake Shack

"Hospitality is central to the restaurant business, yet it's a hard idea to define precisely. Mostly, it involves being nice to people and making them feel welcome. You notice it when it's there, and you particularly notice it when it isn't. A single significant lapse in this area can be your dominant impression of an entire meal."

John Lanchester

Eating is not merely a material pleasure. Eating well gives a spectacular joy to life and contributes immensely to goodwill and happy companionship. It is of great importance to the morale

Elsa Schiaparelli

12. "Growing Old"

It happens to all of us—we grow old. And as I grow older, I think of Clint Eastwood who said it best when he said: *A man's got to know his limitations.* I can't tell you how many times I've hurt myself trying to do something that I used to be able to do, but am just not fast enough, strong enough, or fit enough to do it now.

My blood pressure shot up to 164.
It's never been anywhere near this before.
I made an appointment, to go and see doc.
He checked me all over, then started to talk:

I want you to exercise more every day,
By joining the gym or the YMCA.
There's one other change now that you'll need to make,
You'll need to cut back on the salt you in-take.

I went nearly salt-free—severely cut back,
And ran on the treadmill and jogged 'round the track.
My hard work paid off, as my blood pressure eased.
I went back to doc and was he ever pleased!

But just when I thought I was healthy once more,
My radial nerve became pinched and got sore.
My surgeon prepared me for my big ordeal;
Describing incisions, and how I would feel.

I'm learning to cope with my post-op constraints;
The cast, and my arm sling, and all my complaints.
My stitches come out of my arm in a week.
The chances of pain-free that day's lookin' bleak.

It's hard to remember this stuff going on,
When I was a bulletproof lad made of brawn.
The next generation needs facts yet untold,
Forget what you've heard, it's a bitch growing old.

"It is not true that people stop pursuing dreams because they grow old, they grow old because they stop pursuing dreams."

Gabriel García Márquez

"I believe that the greatest gift you can give your family and the world is a healthy you."

Joyce Meyer

Melissa Coutu - *I really enjoyed this poem. I'm 31 years old, and you're right, growing old is a bitch. Nicely penned.*

Social Outcast - *Haha. I don't want to grow old. Each line of this poem had its own humor. I enjoyed reading it!*

RiskRat - *I know the feeling! Got a hernia operation next week. This is a well-constructed poem with good humor. Nicely written.*

Richom - *Terrific, both in construction and content. All of us older geezers on this site recognize and endure much the same. It's one problem after another.*

Sequestered - *You're a detailed inker and most certainly a deep thinker. You sure write and make your readers non-blinkers. Another impressively inked poem I'm reading from you. Great post.*

Mlou - *Well told and rhymed! I sure can agree with that!! I just spent last night in the ER with BP over 200 and AFIB kicking up. It's hell growing old, but let's face it, it's better than the alternative.*

wishintreeUK - *This is another of your poetic creations I have read and thoroughly enjoyed. You seem to have a natural talent for rhyme. The title is of course very apt for this particular write, with imagery which creates a strong, effective word picture for your reader to experience and enjoy. From experience, this really made me smile. Very well done. Thank you for sharing your poem. Enjoyed it.*

13. "Back off Young-ins"

I grew up in Wilmington, Delaware. Although most of us moved away after high school, many of my close friends returned to Wilmington after college and began working in various jobs around town.

After I retired in Dallas, I created a Bucket List. One of my top desires was to re-connect with my high school friends back in Delaware. So once a year, I would schedule a trip back to see my former classmates.

It always made me feel welcome when friends would gather at a downtown live jazz club to hold a get-together on my behalf. During most of the gatherings, my friend the owner, asked me if I would like to sit in on the drums. If I hadn't been a country western drummer, I might have gone ahead and joined the jazz band for a number or two.

In addition to having live Jazz music, they offered an open mike opportunity where folks could get up and sing, tell jokes, or read poetry. Even though I never actually participated in the open mike entertainment, I dreamed about doing so upon my return to Texas. I had this vivid dream of an audience of Millennials expecting me to recite my poetry while acting it out in a kind of Shakespearean style. Instead, I was standing there motionless, reading glasses hanging from the tip of my nose, simply reading my poetry. In my dream, the audience was just staring at me. I woke up in a fitful sweat.

Young folks like you can remember,
The words of the poems that you write.
You can recite verse with nary a note,
While I must keep my poems in sight.

Even though you guys have mem'ries,
We never will give up or quit.
Seniors are able to do many things,
We just can't remember much shit.

"When old people speak it is not because of the sweetness of words in our mouths; it is because we see something which you do not see."

Chinua Achebe

"It had long since come to my attention that people of accomplishment rarely sat back and let things happen to them. They went out and happened to things."

Leonardo Da Vinci

- *"Abraham Lincoln was 52 when he became president.*
- *Ray Kroc was 53 when he bought the McDonalds Franchise.*
- *Dr. Seuss was 54 when he wrote The Cat in the Hat.*
- *Chesley "Sully" Sullenberger III was 57 when he successfully ditched US Airways Flight 1549 in the Hudson River in 2009.*
- *Colonel Harland Sanders was 61 when he started KFC.*
- *J.R.R Tolkien was 62 when the Lord of the Ring books came out.*
- *Ronald Reagan was 69 when he became President of the US.*
- *Jack Lalane at age 70, handcuffed and shackled, towed 70 rowboats.*
- *Nelson Mandela was 76 when he became President.*
- Leonardo Da Vinci was 51 when he painted the Mona Lisa."

Pablo

"Old people love to give good advice; it compensates them for their inability to set a bad example."

Francois de La Rochefoucauld

"I have a wonderful respect for old people."

Craig Kilborn

"After a lifetime of working, raising families, and contributing to the success of this nation in countless other ways, senior citizens deserve to retire with dignity."

Charlie Gonzalez

14. "A Tribute to Merle Haggard"

Merle Haggard is perhaps my all-time favorite country western singer. I've followed his career for as long as I can remember. His biography is so interesting. I've watched his YouTube videos, purchased all of his music, and bought several DVDs of his live performances. I've even danced the two-step to his music. There are few really great country acts whose music lasts for decades to come. Merle Haggard is one of them.

I've deep love for music, especially Haggard's.
It started with Beach Boy's, The Beatles', and Jagger's.
Then Patsy, Kristofferson, Jennings, and Tucker,
To Paycheck, Dwight Yoakam, and Darius Rucker.

I listen to Blackhawk, George Jones, and Wade Bowen,
Brad Paisley, The Mavericks, Pat Green, and Jake Owen.
I missed the Las Vegas Faith Hill and McGraw show,
But witnessed George Strait cut his, *Come on Joe* demo.

I've never seen Buck at his own Crystal Palace,
And Dave Alan Coe is so terribly callous.
But met Larry Stewart and Miss Antebellum;
Snuck in to see Lonestar, but please never tell 'em.

Attended a gig with the group Shenandoah,
And met Marty Raybon back stage at Club Boa.
This happened before he went Gospel and Bluegrass,
Heard *Bubba Can Dance*; I thought, *this song will kick-ass*.

I saw Reckless Kelley at Gruene Hall last summer.
At Mozie's, I met him—the Buster Jiggs drummer.
Forgive me for skipping ole Leonard and Lefty,
There's too many great acts to write about deftly.

Imagine if there were no San Quentin Merle;
No Bakersfield sound, and no snaps made of pearl.
He's influenced Biaz, Garcia—whole genres,
Yet, no one's come close to Hag's Best-in-Class honors.

"We need to have music that contributes to the well-being of the spirit. Music that cradles people's lives and makes things a little easier. That's what I try to do, and what I want to do. You don't want to close the door on hope."

"By the time you get close to the answers, it's nearly all over."

"Lay in the weeds and wait, and when you get your chance to say something, say something good."

"Faith is the only way we're going to make it. None of us are smart enough to do it on our own."

"The only thing that I miss lately in all music is somebody that will put out a melody that you can whistle. It doesn't seem like there's anything happening like that."

"Running down on a way of life our fighting men have fought and died to keep. If you don't love it, leave it."

"Willie Nelson's the one who told me the reason it costs so much to get divorced is because it's worth it."

"Keep your opinions to yourself. I think it's important that I stay neutral on politics and remain hard to understand. I don't want to be pigeonholed as conservative, liberal, independent or anything. I back the man for the things the man believes in, not whether it says "R" or "D" down there beside his name."

"It sounds like something from a Woody Guthrie song, but it's true; I was raised in a freight car."

Merle Haggard

"You know, legends are people like Haggard and Jones and Wills and Sinatra. Those people are legends. I'm just a young buck out here trying to keep in that same circle with the rest of 'em."

George Strait

15. "Thinker or Feeler?"

I've realized for much of my life now, that women are much more sensitive and emotional than men. But I'm quite sure that I still don't comprehend the full extent of the sensitivity chasm that exists between us thinkers and those feelers. But people change.

Thinker or feeler? Which are you, my man?
You better be thinking as much as you can.
Girls are the feelers, much more so than men.
They're feeling all day and then feeling again.

Truth being told though, we guys can feel too,
But never confess all the times we feel blue.
Little by little, we stuff blue things down,
Emerging in time, as a Sad-Happy-Clown.

Once in a lifetime a girl comes along,
Who causes a thinker to see he's been wrong.
Tenderly caring, she thaws out his heart.
And shows him a new way to feel and take part.

Since he has changed some, he feels like a child.
And sensing her love now, his heart's running wild.
Realizing treasure he longs to pursue,
He eagerly tells her: *I'll always love you!*

"Love is friendship that has caught fire. It is quiet understanding, mutual confidence, sharing and forgiving. It is loyalty through good and bad times. It settles for less than perfection and makes allowances for human weaknesses."

Ann Landers

"Doubt thou the stars are fire, Doubt that the sun doth move. Doubt truth to be a liar, But never doubt I love."

William Shakespeare

"Spread love everywhere you go: first of all in your own house. Give love to your children, to your wife or husband, to a next door neighbor. Let no one ever come to you without leaving feeling better and happier. Be the living expression of God's kindness; kindness in your face, kindness in your eyes, kindness in your smile, kindness in your warm greeting."

Mother Theresa

"Now a soft kiss—Aye, by that kiss, I vow an endless bliss."

John Keats

"She wasn't exactly sure when it happened. Or even when it started. All she knew for sure was that right here and now, she was falling hard and she could only pray that he was feeling the same way."

Nicholas Sparks, Safe Haven

"Love will find a way through paths where wolves fear to prey."

Lord Byron

"A kiss makes the heart young again and wipes out the years."

Rupert Brooke

"If you have only one smile in you, give it to the people you love."

Maya Angelou

"Love is our true destiny. We do not find the meaning of life by ourselves alone—we find it with another."

Thomas Merton

16. "Organized"

I'm different—that's for sure. Some say I'm a neat freak, while others call me particular. But my favorite is when someone acknowledges that I'm simply organized and thorough.

Before I retired, I always had the neatest desk, got reports in on time, arrived at work at precisely the same time every day, and generally left for home every day on a very predictable schedule. You can bet that the folks who worked with me, had fun teasing me about my fastidious ways.

My most interesting revelation however, came to me when I put it together that my superiors always seemed to delegate the most important projects to me, presumably because they knew beyond a shadow of a doubt, that I would bring the projects in on time and under budget. For that, my colleagues showed me respect.

When I was a bach'lor and lived all alone,
My stuff out of order, I could not condone.
Not one jot or tittle allowed out of place,
Disorderly living I thought a disgrace.

My colleagues at work though, seemed polar from me;
Appearing haphazard like slapdash times three.
The bane of their workday, they still had respect,
They envied my anal retentive effect.

"Getting organized in the normal routines of life and finishing little projects you've started is an important first step toward realizing larger goals. If you can't get a handle on the small things, how will you ever get it together to focus on the big things?"

Joyce Meyer

"Science is organized knowledge. Wisdom is organized life."

Immanuel Kant

17. "Another New Year's Resolution"

Everyone's done this; made a serious, heartfelt and very much needed New Year's Resolution in order to improve themselves, only to lose interest, fail to accomplish their goal, and then roll over the very same New Year's Resolution to the following new year. Succinctly put, I will do this year what I promised to do last year.

Jack and Jill just joined a gym
'Cause they were 10 pounds bigger.
Jack chose weights and Jill chose skates,
Both filled with vim and vigor.

Painful were those first few days
Of pumping iron and skating.
Big Jack moaned and poor Jill groaned,
But there was no abating.

Breezing through their first ten months,
Each getting strong and thinner,
Both thought they would meet or beat
Their goals and be a winner.

Never ending pumps and strides,
They envied being care-free.
We need breaks, for Heaven's sakes,
Let's stop for roasted turkey.

They would ponder this short pause,
Thanksgiving fast approaching.
Jack asked, *Could?*, and Jill said, *Should!*
Was idleness encroaching?

Next time they were at the gym
Their trainer weighed their asses.
Jack scaled more; gained pounds galore,
And Jill'd increased her masses.

Beaten down yet born again,
Embarrassed by their actions,
Both worked hard displacing lard,
Ignoring all distractions.

Shedding pounds and getting fit
And burning every fat cell,
Christmas came and strict turned lame.
Their muscles morphed to soft gel.

Victims, pulled both left and right,
Confounded by the seasons.
Life's too short, our fun to thwart,
They reasoned, without reasons.

Not to end with Jack and Jill's
Failed over-weight solutions,
There's a way, to save their day:
Fresh New Year's Resolutions.

"Physical fitness is not only one of the most important keys to a healthy body, it is the basis of dynamic and creative intellectual activity."

John F. Kennedy

"The new year stands before us, like a chapter in a book, waiting to be written. We can help write that story by setting goals."

Melody Beattie

princess wulfa - *We all need to improve ourselves one way or the other. Thank you for sharing this write. It was a lot of fun to read it. This made me smile. I think we've all done this before. Very entertaining and enjoyable read. Thank you.*

18. "In the Beginning"

Sometimes you meet that special person and you're changed forever. You have new and exciting feelings. You see the world differently. You've changed. You're in love.

I can't figure out, I'm baffled no doubt,
This thing makes me feel like a wreck.
You call on the phone, I'm chilled to the bone,
The hair's standing up on my neck.

You send me a note, I've lumps in my throat,
And radiance beams from my face.
You walk in a room, my heart rate goes zoom,
Composure is gone—not a trace.

We start holding hands, my heart, it expands,
I wonder what's happened to me?
You wrap me in hugs, I think I'm on drugs,
I never have felt this carefree.

Before our first date, I'm anxious—can't wait,
My nerves almost out of control.
You kiss my warm cheek, my knees—they go weak,
I'm glowing from deep in my soul.

Our lips start to touch, I grab you—we clutch,
My feet start to lift off the ground.
The next thing I know, it's late—time to go.
My life has just changed, I had found.

I get home amazed, in love and half crazed,
So much for me taking it slow.
The very next day, I wake up and pray,
God, thank you for blessing me so.

"There is only one happiness in this life, to love and be loved."

George Sand

"Truelove is like ghosts, which everyone talks about and few have seen."

Francois de La Rochefoucauld

"Wind power, water power, coal power. How great would it be if you could harness the power of a young man in love?"

Richard Dahm

"Stardust sails endless distances through the silent ages until, white-hot, it strikes a ready heart."

Terri Guillemets

"You can't blame gravity for falling in love."

Albert Einstein

"We never get enough of falling in love and believing in love."

Shemar Moore

"The course of true love never did run smooth."

William Shakespeare, A Midsummer Night's Dream

"He's not your prince if he doesn't make sure you know that you're his princess."

Demi Lovato

"True love is the best thing in the world, except for cough drops."

William Goldman, The Princess Bride

19. "The Moody Princess"

Some time ago, I was sitting in a hot tub on a cruise ship talking to a fellow passenger. He was telling me all about his recent experiences with his wife, who was going through menopause. On one hand, his story was entertaining, but on the other hand, it was eye-opening and quite sad, as many women have to deal with some very dramatic, life altering hormonal changes. He said that just months ago, she was a real princess; wonderful in every way. Then all of a sudden, without warning, she became moody and argumentative. He and his wife, train, breed, board, and sell Thoroughbred horses on their large horse farm outside of West Chester, Pennsylvania. I wish them both the best, as they work through this difficult time, and I thank them for the inspiration I needed in order to write this poem. I hope they're doing well!

Princesses come and then princesses go.
Some you have heard of, but some you don't know.
Once, they wore clothing that set them apart;
Always the finest, like Rembrandt's fine art.

Time's, they are changing, and princesses too.
Now one can't tell who exactly is who.
Only the wisest of wise men discerns,
Who is a princess and who merely yearns.

Many have talked about one in the east.
One day she's royal; the next day a beast.
Why do they think that this princess is real?
Meet her one time—it's so hard to conceal.

How could a girl be half sweet and half bitch?
Surely you've heard of that estrogen glitch!
Princesses older than say, fifty-nine,
Need help from hormones to keep moods in line.

Many a man wants to find her one day.
I were a gambler? I'd bet on PA.
Not around Pittsburgh, but farther southeast.
Stop when you see lots of four-legged beast.

Finding her won't be a real easy task.
Listen to me and you'll know what to ask.
Search for a beauty who has lots of class,
Acting like she has a bug up her ass.

"Always remember that you are absolutely unique. Just like everyone else."

Margaret Mead

"I'm sorry, if you were right, I'd agree with you."

Robin Williams

"Any girl can be glamorous. All you have to do is stand still and look stupid."

Hedy Lamarr

"I call the Change of Life Orchids because menopause is such an ugly word. It's got men in it for god sakes."

"When I was suddenly thrust into what everyone calls menopause earlier than my body planned, I decided someone needed to take charge on so many levels. It was time to speak up and say Hey! This isn't an old lady's disease! We aren't old! We are strong and dammit, we are beautiful and sexy too!"

Lisa Jey Davis

"The more you worry, the more you throw off the delicate balance of hormones required for health."

Andrew J. Bernstein

"I can be a bit grumpy. I'm full of angst, and hormones."

Nicholas Hoult

20. "Those Damn Books"

Have you ever seen a child misbehaving at the mall? The parent either gives in to what their kid wants, or bribes the kid with promises of food or gifts. I rarely if ever, have seen a misbehaving child get spanked or punished in some meaningful way. It seems that the older I get, the more I witness this scenario. So I thought that as a grandfather, I have the right and maybe the responsibility, to express my disappointment in these parents and their children. I wonder if they've ever heard of tough love?

Whine Your Way to Victory.
Read only by pre-teens.
Every other kid now'days
Has mastered its routines.

Author's penned them one more tome:
A Guide For Causing Strife.
That's why moms are so strung out
And wish they had a life.

Manners and respect in kids,
Are traits we seldom see.
Save those boys in Beaver's clan,
And Rockwell's artistry.

Sparing rod will spoil a child;
A fact that folks ignore.
Why can't parents discipline
And spank kids once, or more?

Parents love their kids so much,
They strive to be their friend.
Truth is young-ins need some rules;
But rules that do not bend.

Don't they know that they might raise
A selfish, spoiled brat?
Parents change and come around,
But I don't bet on that.

What can gramps and granny do;
Observe and bide our time?
Shrink of mine says journaling,
Or writing smart-ass rhyme.

"The world is being run by irresponsible spoiled brats."

P. J. O'Rourke

"I'm so spoiled—I must have a Starbucks vanilla latte every day."

Katie Holmes

"A happy childhood has spoiled many a promising life."

Robertson Davies

"I was quite the spoiled brat. I have quite a temper, obviously inherited from my father, and I became very good at ordering everyone around. I was the princess; the staff were absolutely terrified of me."

Lisa Marie Presley

"The baby boomers are the most spoiled, most self-centered, most narcissistic generation the country's ever produced."

Stephen Bannon

"Kids raised to be pampered and spoiled don't really end up being good leaders. Leaders need to be independent minded and confident."

Amy Chua

21. "Our Little Angel from Above"

One of the most dramatic and impressive displays of Christian faith I've ever witnessed was when my stepdaughter and her husband were trying to conceive a child. They tried and tried and tried with no success. They went to every kind of doctor they could think of. Still nothing. Finally, they just stopped in their tracks and prayed together. They told God that they would very much like to have a child, but it just didn't seem to be in His plan for their lives. They ended their prayer by vowing that no matter what God decided to do about giving them a baby, they would continue to praise Him for His enduring love and faithfulness. And guess what? A month later my stepdaughter was pregnant.

We waited and waited and waited some more.
We couldn't just go to the *New-Baby-Store*.
The wine was uncorked,
We watched for the stork,
Not patiently waiting; but pacing the floor.

Expecting our girl to be perfect, we prayed,
Outgoing, real smart, and just never afraid.
But needless to say,
Prepared we were—nay,
For prayers that He answered—our faith not betrayed.

While watching and helping our girl grow and grow,
Our hearts became brilliantly, brighter aglow.
We couldn't have guessed,
How much we'd been blessed,
By God up in Heaven, from where blessings flow.

We wonder what kind of a girl she will be.
I guess we'll just wait and then someday we'll see.
But one thing's for sure,
When grown and mature,
She'll follow You Lord and for that we thank Thee.

22. "I'm Deeply Disappointed"

My wife and I had been attending a big church for years but had never assimilated into the church family. So one day we decided to join a bible study class. First we tried a big group for all ages, then another and another, until we finally decided on a smaller class of folks our own age. We were faithful in our attendance, but week after week we went home uninspired and disappointed. We discussed this unexpected situation for weeks before finally deciding that this particular group of church goers were fake Christians. They were as the Bible says, Pharisees. So we quit, and found ourselves a real group of Christians to fellowship and study with.

It's: *Clearly, in so much as,*
Those words you rarely hear,
Except in bloviation,
At pubs, partaking beer.

Folks talking like they're better,
All others they besmirch.
We never thought we'd hear this
In Sunday School or church.

That's what we always figured,
Until that fateful day.
We went to class to study;
To learn, to grow, to pray.

Our classmates sounded shallow;
A bent to play the game.
That's not what we expected.
In fact, 'twas pretty lame.

Repeating Christian doctrine,
As in a play—on cue;
Not letting us inside them,
Or letting them show through.

We tried to get to know them,
But could not figure out,
The reason they pretended;
What were they all about?

So opening ole Webster
To see what friendship meant,
We found out what we'd figured;
It's rare; some say God-sent.

I guess it's time for change now;
This did not work out well.
It steals our peace to be there;
They all can go to hell.

"Hypocrites in the Church? Yes, and in the lodge and at the home. Don't hunt through the Church for a hypocrite. Go home and look in the mirror. Hypocrites? Yes. See that you make the number one less."

Billy Sunday

"I think, to me, reality is better than being fake."

Ice Cube

"You got nothing to lose. You don't lose when you lose fake friends."

Joan Jett

"Fake relationships and fake people coming up to me and all of a sudden wanting to be my friend."

Jason Ritter

23. "Another Dinner Party"

Here's a story about a small dinner party that we recently hosted. It was really a lot of fun, as everyone was in a very jovial mood. But as with every single other time we had guests over to the house, my wife insisted upon a series of picture taking in various areas of the house and in several poses, before anyone was allowed to leave. The women loved the photo shoot. The men, not so much. But it was always mandatory.

My wife prepared Poppy-Seed Chicken.
Guests hungry, their chops they were lickin'.
They ate more and more,
Till feeling quite sore,
'Cause mid-riffs had started to thicken.

It's lucky we ever got seated.
Although chair assignments completed,
Sir Dean moved by Prue,
Anita by Sue,
And out of her throne Pat was cheated.

We finished our dinner then talked more,
Told stories and laughed—what an uproar!
But when time to go,
Patricia said, *No!*
Not yet before pictures are posed for.

"As we grow up, we learn that the people that weren't supposed to ever let us down, probably will. You'll have your heart broken and you'll break others hearts. You'll blame a new love for things an old one did. You'll fight with your best friend, and you'll cry because time is flying by, and eventually you'll lose someone you love. So take too many pictures, laugh too much, forgive freely, and love like you've never been hurt. Because every second you spend angry or upset, is a second of happiness you can never get back."

Anonymous

24. "A Star Shines on Max"

Max is one of my grandchildren. I'll never forget how loving he's been from the time he was about two years old, right up to the present day. I've never really seen anything like it. It's truly amazing.

We see it all around us,
Our young begin to grow.
We call it maturation,
But sometimes I don't know.

I see adults around me,
Who've never really grown.
Maturity they're lacking,
But why, is yet unknown.

I think it has to do with
A trait I see in Max.
He's learned to love all others,
A trait vain mankind lacks.

He's sweet and kind and loving,
His hugs so deeply felt.
Each time I hold and hug him
My heart begins to melt.

How is it that he's learned to
Love family and his friends?
So tenderly he loves them.
His love, from where, transcends?

You want to learn the answer?
You need not look too far.
The one who's taught Max loving?
His mother—she's the star!

"It is the Holy Spirit's job to convict, God's job to judge and my job to love."

Billy Graham

25. "The Entertaining 2016 Primaries"

The 2016 primaries were really a hoot. It seemed to me that they didn't so much represent the civilized democratic process that we might have all expected, but were more of a cross between a prize fight and a three-ring circus. I was so entertained by all of the players during that time, that I thought I'd try to capture the essence of the primaries in this poem.

Of all the fine folks that are running,
Sir Trump seems to wield all the cunning.
He fights with Ted Cruz,
They hit hard; they bruise,
But Trump's prolonged winning is stunning.

The rest of the pack, although bragging;
Their poll numbers just keep on lagging.
It's Marco alone,
Who's striving; its known,
To rise up with efforts unflagging.

While Hillary's battling Bernie,
The FBI's on their own journey.
They're searching for crimes,
Revealing at times,
That Hillary needs an attorney.

Now Bernie's another strange story.
When speaking, he seems in his glory.
But things that he's said,
Have filled some with dread.
His ways are too regulatory.

So who's going to win these tough races,
And occupy choice White House spaces?
It's just not real clear,
But as time grows near,
We may seek Joe Biden's good graces.

"Elections remind us of the rights and responsibilities of citizenship in a democracy."

Robert Kennedy

"Voting is how we participate in a civic society—be it for president, be it for a municipal election. It's the way we teach our children—in school elections—how to be citizens, and the importance of their voice."

Loretta Lynch

"Put a lawn sign on your lawn; go door to door. Register people to vote. There's so much we can do through our voices and time. That's what flips elections."

Kirsten Gillibrand

"Is the purpose of free elections to allow the most clever and vicious person to aggregate power, or is the purpose of free elections to enable the American people to have a serious conversation about their country's future and try to find both a policy and a personality that they think will carry to them that better future?"

Newt Gingrich

"One of the reasons people hate politics is that truth is rarely a politician's objective. Election and power are."

Cal Thomas

Richom - *Excellent rhyme, metered limericks, and sadly, all too true. It seems that all of the 2016 candidates were badly damaged. As for who will almost surely defeat Trump in 2020, I hope for a well-qualified, fresh face rather than an old retread like Biden.*

Stayathomepoet - *This gave me a good laugh! I feel as though you cleverly summarized the 2016 election. I look forward to a poem summarizing the current President's first and only term. Nice work!*

26. "A Genuine, Godly Love"

Sandy was married some 38 years before she found out that her loving husband had been sleeping around for a long, long time. As if that realization wasn't devastating enough, she was forced to endure a nightmare of a divorce. She was powerless to fight the demise of her long-term marriage. Then we met, and we were both smitten.

Oh Sandy, sweet Sandy, from whence did you come?
The day that we met, my heart beat like a drum.
I think you're from Heaven, not North Texas towns,
For Heaven alone awards halo-type crowns.

You wear yours so well and 'twas honestly earned.
You came down to earth and you've not yet returned.
Like Jesus, you've hurt and you've cried many tears.
But power's returned now—you harbor no fears.

So how did you come to choose this lowly man?
'Cause you could choose anyone; Lord knows you can.
I think God arranged it and blessed me so much.
I know that He did, 'cause I know His sweet touch.

Dear Sandy, I love you with all of my heart.
I pray that we'll wed and we never will part.
The best thing that's happened, just happened to me.
For that I thank you dear, and also thank Thee!

"Truelove, to me, is when she's the first thought that goes through your head when you wake up and the last thought that goes through your head before you go to sleep."

Justin Timberlake

"Live simply, love generously, care deeply, and leave the rest to God."

Ronald Reagan

Show me your scars. Show me the most damaged parts of you And I promise that I will take care of you for always. I promise that I will sit with your hands in mine even when the stars go out.

Jyoti Patel, The Curved Rainbow

"We all want to be happy and feel valued. We want love, connection, respect, health, vitality, passion, and success. When you generously provide these emotions for others, you activate the law of attraction to magnetize the same experiences for you."

Susan C. Young

"Evidence of a heart touched by God's grace is a heart overflowing with generosity."

Gary Rohrmayer

"All around us are the miracles of God. A tiny seed grows into a peepul tree. A caterpillar becomes a butterfly!"

Dada J.P. Vaswani

"God does not speak in any regional language, national language and international language, he speaks in the language of love"

Jagadeesh Kumar

PrttyBrd - *Great love story. I love the romance and the meant-to-be feel of it.*

Ice Brat - *I can feel it through you, but I have never known it.*

princess wulfa - *Love it, to get that love once in a lifetime, to come into your life, is an amazing and very beautiful thing. I wish everybody could experience it just once, be it just for a little while. Beautiful poem. Well written. Really enjoyed it. Thank you. Nicely penned.*

27. "My Dear, Sweet Granddaughter"

I actually have two granddaughters. This poem was written for one of them on her birthday, but believe me, they are both as sweet as any granddaughters can be.

Every time I think of you,
I think of sweetness through and through.
A daughter, sister, and a friend.
You're faithful till the bitter end.

Even from the very start,
We knew you had a big warm heart.
You're curious, adventuresome,
There's nothing you can't overcome.

What you have is very rare.
You're smart, sincere, and really care.
Your future's waiting patiently,
As you fulfill your destiny.

Anything you want to do,
You can, and will, if you pursue.
Just don't leave out your God above,
And know that you have all my love.

"Just when you think you know all that love is… along come the grandchildren."

Unknown.

"Grandchildren are loving reminders of what we're really here for."

Janet Lanese

28. "Vacation from Love"

This award-winning poem is a story in rhyme, about a loving couple, just starting out in marriage, full of hopeful anticipation of a blissful life together. Then, life's distractions begin pulling them apart. So, just as they're about to call it quits, they decide to get some marital counseling. Their counselor gives them some very wise and practical advice. It's their choice whether or not they take heed. *Vacation from Love* was awarded AllPoetry's First Place Gold Award for the best poem in its category. And, chosen among many poems to be published by The Society of Classical Poets.

Happily dating for almost two years,
Enjoying our courtship without any tears.
With marriage approaching, I'm bursting with love,
For she is my angel, who's sent from above.

First months of marriage were blissful and dear.
We cherished each other and had a rich year.
But jobs and the kids seemed to get in the way.
We drifted apart more and more every day.

First we were silent, then started to fight.
Our past expectations grew wings and took flight.
We hired a couns'lor and shared all our wrath.
He talked with us both and then laid out a path.

Love is a choice, he said, *work is required.*
You must be attentive, and when you're admired,
You'll start doing things that she loves and she needs.
Then love will grow back and your marriage succeeds.

You, my sweet lady, you must do the same.
And ask your dear husband what sets him aflame.
You'll find when you do, he'll start turning around,
And love will return and will start to abound.

Quality time should be focused and real.
The more time together, the better you'll feel.
Then both should begin giving gifts to your mate.
And soon your resentments will start to abate.

You sir, should start doing some of her chores,
Spontaneous acts of your service endures.
And same for the lady, in love as you are.
Just see what will happen when YOU wash the car.

Terms of endearment are love's little seeds.
Your verbal expressions mean more than good deeds.
So tell her she's pretty and tell her she's sweet.
And tell her her cooking just cannot be beat.

Pointers I've shared will restore what you've lost.
Indeed, when you follow regardless of cost.
With work and some prayer and some help from above,
You'll end your traumatic vacation from love.

"Counseling was amazing, but I didn't know how loved I was until after my marriage had gone through its darkest time."

Sarah Drew

"Sometimes, just the act of venting is helpful. Counseling provides a safe haven for precisely that kind of free-ranging release: You can say things in the therapist's office, with the therapist present, that would be incendiary or hurtful in your living room."

Laura Wasser

Ron Duffie - *It's not every day or even every so often, I read a poem having so many truths from start to finish; & real life-changing remedies. The title should be a household name. And all of its contents should be found with all who desire truelove, friendships, & strategies to better understand their personal virtue. I'm encouraged by this poem which stays the path of truth, & integrity and courageousness. This poet is a real life narrator of heroic proportions. Thanks for sharing—well done!*

Beebs - *I really liked this. Thank you for sharing. Very powerful words, yet very simplistic. It's like learning the ABCs all over again.*

Melissa Coutu - *I can really feel the situation, great poem.*

wishintreeUK - *This is brilliant! The title is spot on, with the introduction leading nicely into the rest of your word picture. Rhyme too, helps tremendously with the flow of your poem making it such a delight to read; nothing is forced. Such words of wisdom which any couple would do well to take note of, if there are problems needing a remedy. Well done. Amazing!*

sealife - *If there was a contest somewhere for great husbands, I bet you would win. And I am sure the woman who inspired you to such great heights would win a contest for great wives. This is a great poem, following the natural stages of relationships phases and how to keep the spark. This poem will be good for many to read. Bravo Poet!*

Sequestered - *You've inked from experience, words of wisdom. Very apt and timely, yet poetically appealing. Nice, enriching.*

Summer Snow - *I feel more than ever, this is a piece I needed to read tonight. This is well written, skillfully rhymed, and speaks volumes to many marriages struggling in today's times. Well done.*

Beautiful Dreamer23 - *This was very great, and very wise how you explained this out. I could tell this came from your heart, and I wish you both the very best as well. This poem was very deep, and great advice through the poem as well. You wrote this out with your heart.*

Hitesh C Bhakat - *It is a beautiful composition with an apt title. A series of vocabulary items builds a picture connoting a sense of harmony and hope amidst disharmony and discord. Having undergone an inexplicable phase in the middle of married life, the narrator seems to have gained an invaluable insight to protect all broken relationship and recount bounty and blessings of the Lord. Nicely penned, created.*

Amethyst Blue -*This was a very lovely post you have penned. I enjoyed the flow and the message of unity between two people; fresh images in burning simplicity and deft brevity in expressions; the precise statement of metaphors adds beauty to the poem. Lovely!*

29. "My Fall from Grace"

This is a story of one guy's misfortune, brought on by his own shortcomings. He clawed his way to the top, then crashed and burned. *And Then*, he finds redemption.

From the soaring great heights of prosperity,
Protected from penniless poverty,
I fell to the depths of debauchery,
Enduring the worst kind of mockery,
Because of my pride and my snobbery.

From the safe and sound space of my comfort zone,
I plunged to despair; I lost all I own.
Because of the seeds that I'd wildly sown,
My future, no doubt, is completely blown.
And now I deserve to just moan and groan.

I was top of the heap; I was bold and brave;
A powerful force, like a mighty wave.
But now just a ripple; a galley slave,
There's no one who cares if I rant or rave.
I'm buried inside a symbolic grave.

So the point of my story, I do believe,
Is, all of my life I have been naive.
Great dangers ahead, I did not perceive,
So, destined I am to forever grieve;
A permanent sentence with no reprieve.

"You must make a decision that you are going to move on. It wont happen automatically. You will have to rise up and say, 'I don't care how hard this is, I don't care how disappointed I am, I'm not going to let this get the best of me. I'm moving on with my life."

Joel Osteen, Your Best Life Now: 7 Steps to Living at Your Full Potential

30. "And Then"

Then Jesus stopped by on His daily walk.
He asked me: *Dear friend, would you like to talk?*
His timing was perfect; I didn't balk.
I promised I'd listen; I wouldn't mock.

But what He was claiming was wild, if true.
I never once heard this; 'twas all brand new.
So why would He care for us lowly few?
No others have stopped; just continued through.

He told me His dad is the God above.
The God of forgiveness, of grace, and love.
He treated me much like a helpless dove.
I yearned to believe but I craved a shove.

So what must I do for redemption then?
Admit you're a sinner, like all saved men.
Then trust Me as Savior and ask of Me,
For grace and forgiveness on bended knee.

"When granted many years of life, growing old in age is natural, but growing old with grace is a choice. Growing older with grace is possible for all who will set their hearts and minds on the Giver of grace, the Lord Jesus Christ."

Billy Graham

"The meaning of life. The wasted years of life. The poor choices of life. God answers the mess of life with one word: grace."

Max Lucado

"Those who dare to fail miserably can achieve greatly."

John F. Kennedy

"The ideal man bears the accidents of life with dignity and grace, making the best of circumstances."

Aristotle

"Infuse your life with action. Don't wait for it to happen. Make it happen. Make your own future. Make your own hope. Make your own love. And whatever your beliefs, honor your Creator, not by passively waiting for grace to come down from upon high, but by doing what you can to make grace happen... yourself, right now, right down here on Earth."

Bradley Whitford

"What gives me the most hope every day is God's grace; knowing that his grace is going to give me the strength for whatever I face, knowing that nothing is a surprise to God."

Rick Warren

"I'm not perfect. And who knows how many times I've fallen short. We all fall short. That's the amazing thing about the grace of God."

Tim Tebow

"Failure is the condiment that gives success its flavor."

Truman Capote

Felonious Monk - *A humbling fall from grace. The summit of highs, followed by a valley of lows. It happens to the very best. Great flow and message. Nicely done!*

Jan Serene - *Wow. Just WOW! I don't even know what to say, but I'll try. Your end rhymes are so perfectly placed and not forced. You tell a sad story of a man awakening to the true meaning of life but feeling it's too late to make amends. Actually put tears in my eyes. So glad I found you here, poet.*

31. "Happy Birthday Dear Sandy"

Sandy's mother used to call Sandy every year on her birthday. She'd describe her wonderful memory of the first time she ever saw her sweet little baby girl in the hospital. Sandy grew to love and cherish that story, and she would eagerly anticipate her mother's birthday call every year. When her mother went to heaven, the calls stopped. That left a huge hole in Sandy's heart, until one day, Sandy realized that her mother continues telling her that very same story through prayer. Now, Sandy tells it to us.

Happy birthday dear Sandy.
Expecting that call;
It came early those mornings,
The best call of all!

I remember so clearly,
The story she'd tell.
'Bout the first time she saw me,
She told it so well.

Seeing nurses approaching
Her hospital bed,
Trusted arms brought a newborn,
Wrapped toes to her head.

Then so sweetly she gave me
To anxious, dear mom,
And the look on her face was
Ecstatic—yet calm.

But when mom went to heaven,
The calls, they did cease.
Now in prayer does she call me,
And that gives me peace.

"It may not always be easy, but you're the love of my life. My heart is riding on a runaway train, you are the love of my life. Through all the pleasure and pain, from the moment I first saw you, I knew that you were the love of my life."

Carly Simon

32. "My Broken Heart"

I was sitting on an airplane a long time ago, next to a gentleman who was visibly upset. I wasn't sure whether to ask him if everything was okay or not. So I decided to try and make him feel a little bit better by introducing myself and seeing if he wanted to chat. What resulted, was like a dam bursting through its walls. He began telling me the sad, sad story of how his fiancé not only broke his heart, but thoroughly stomped all over it, and then kicked it to the curb. This poem was written to express this guy's absolute emotional destruction.

Just laying in bed,
Third day in a row.
He hurt from his head,
Right down to his toe.

The girl he would wed,
He trusted her so.
She loved him, she said,
But also loved Joe.

Completely misled,
His heart was aglow.
And now he feels dead;
She cheats like a pro.

The truth? Not a thread.
So how could he know,
That her legs were spread,
For more than one beau?

I pray he will shed
This foreboding low,
And one day instead,
Find truelove and grow.

"You didn't just cheat on me; you cheated on us. You didn't just break my heart; you broke our future."

Steve Maraboli, Unapologetically You

"I don't know why they call it heartbreak. It feels like every other part of my body is broken too."

Unknown

"Until this moment, I had not realized that someone could break your heart twice, along the very same fault lines."

Jodi Picoult, My Sister's Keeper

"I think many people can relate to that excruciating pain of love gone wrong. I'd rather have a broken arm than a broken heart."

Christie Brinkley

"Hearts can break. Yes, hearts can break. Sometimes I think it would be better if we died when they did, but we don't."

Stephen King

Jan Serene - *Heartache is the worst kind of pain because there's no pill and no cure but time. Great write. You absolutely accomplished telling a meaningful story in beautiful rhyme. I'm so sorry. Please know you're not alone. I've felt this same excruciating pain before and totally understand.*

RiskRat - *What a sad poem. I know I shouldn't, but I like the naughty line best.*

princess wulfa - *That is so sad, but again, that's life. Some people just don't give a damn about hurting and cheating on someone. And it is heart breaking to find yourself in a situation like that. You feel like your whole world is falling apart, and you think life will never get better. Life will go on, and it does get better, although at the time, you don't think it ever will. Good write. Well done. Nicely penned.*

Kavita Jain - *This one is really painful, and your kindness is really beautiful. Hope it helped him well. Inspired me.*

33. "The Worst Kind of Betrayal"

I sat by a guy recently on a return trip from LA. Widowed after 18 years of marriage, he said he felt like Rip Van Winkle, in that he just woke up after a long, long absence from dating, to a brand new world order. For one thing, he said it's very difficult to meet single women at his age. Where does he go, what does he say? Seems like the dating websites are the only platforms available to him for possibly finding truelove.

He told me that every single woman he's met so far, who professed a strong faith in God, seemed to be able to live both a faithful life at church, as well as a worldly life of lying, cheating, deception, and betrayal when dating.

Personally, I haven't had a broken heart for as long as I can remember, but I've had some broken bones and injuries. In this poor guy's opinion, physical pain and suffering, pale in comparison to the pain of a broken heart due to betrayal.

Every single ship of ours,
Is sailing on a sea of lies.
Every single love we share,
Will drown beneath sea's cheating skies.

Every single girl he's met,
Has played him for a total fool.
Every single lie they've told,
Intended to be shrewd and cruel.

Every single time he hurt,
He lost his way, and ceased to feel.
Every single therapist,
Said, take some time and you will heal.

Brokenness, they say, is good;
Enables growth within our hearts.
Every single time we mend,
We pave the way for brand new starts.

Sounds real good but you're not me.
Hey, I'm the one who got betrayed.
Why'd they have to hurt me so,
And carry on their masquerade?

Sadness helped reveal his heart,
Since that's when feelings seem to flow.
He will heal; in time forget,
But he's been told, that trust comes slow.

Pray for her, and not for him,
For one day soon he'll be okay.
She's the one that needs our prayers,
She needs to love and not betray.

"Everyone suffers at least one bad betrayal in their lifetime. It's what unites us. The trick is not to let it destroy your trust in others when that happens. Don't let them take that from you."

Sherrilyn Kenyon, Invincible

"You want to believe that there's one relationship in life that's beyond betrayal. A relationship that's beyond that kind of hurt. And there isn't."

Caleb Carr

Vaishkhushi - *First of all, this is a masterpiece in itself. Secondly, this is a really heartfelt write, and I truly loved reading it. Great.*

Jliles - *Love is a dangerous feeling. Especially when it's not taken when given.*

Brandon Matuja - *What a wonderfully flowing, rhyming, broken-hearted-love poem. Keep writing! This poem resonates with me as a young lady whom I was seeing made it clear that she doesn't want to be close to me anymore. Inspired.*

Daniel11714 - *A hurting soul writes in depth. Excellent piece. Your pain is very clear.*

34. "Help! I've got Writer's Block"

The generally accepted definition of writer's block is, that a formerly prolific writer becomes unable to write anything he deems worthwhile. This condition causes a creative slowdown and ultimately, the writer stops writing all together.

There have been numerous famous writers throughout history who have suffered from writer's block. Some, recovered and went on to write again successfully, while others stopped writing entirely.

With just a couple of new poems left for me to write in order to finally finish my book, I couldn't think of a darn thing to write about. I wrestled with this dead-head feeling for about three weeks before I realized that my next new poem was already half written in my head. I reasoned, that if I'm going to be plagued by writer's block, why not write my next new poem about writer's block? So I did.

Oh, why can't I think of a new poem to write?
I've toiled all-day-long and then into the night.
I've wracked my poor brain but the words won't come out.
I can't even think; I just sit here and pout.

But one of these days I'll come up with a theme;
They come in a thought, or perhaps in a dream.
When I get inspired, I'll start writing some text.
First stanza complete, I'll go on to the next.

It might be a love poem, they're so very sweet.
Or maybe some comedy; that would be neat.
I like writing lim'ricks, they're easy to read.
I'll need to decide though, before I proceed.

Epiphanies come, but I never know when.
So never, I'm far from my pad and my pen.
But sometimes however, they don't come at all,
And then I just sit here and stare at the wall.

It's never been this hard to write a new poem.
It's not as if writing a Michener-esque tome.
If I had a wish, I would wish for a muse,
Creatively speaking, I've nothing to lose.

If I had a muse I'd put Shakespeare to shame.
I'd earn lots of dough and a great deal of fame.
But muse-less I am, not to mention uptight.
Oh, why can't I think of a new poem to write?

"Writing about a writer's block is better than not writing at all."

Charles Bukowski

"The secret of getting ahead is getting started. The secret of getting started is breaking your complex overwhelming tasks into small manageable tasks, and starting on the first one."

Mark Twain

"When I'm writing, I write. And then it's as if the muse is convinced that I'm serious and says, Okay. Okay. I'll come."

Maya Angelou

"I think writer's block is simply the dread that you are going to write something horrible. But as a writer, I believe that if you sit down at the keys long enough, sooner or later something will come out."

Roy Blount, Jr.

"There's no such thing as writer's block. That was invented by people in California who couldn't write."

Terry Pratchett

35. "Parking's a Pain in the Butt"

Everyone I know in Dallas, complains about the stifling heat during our scorching, humid summers. And when they're not complaining about the heat, they're complaining about the unbelievably horrendous traffic we have here on our roads and highways every day; especially during rush hour. But I think what aggravates folks the most in Dallas, is that wherever their destination happens to be, usually there's no place to park.

There's lots of ways to park a car.
It just depends how good you are.
We've all been parking most our life,
And all those years, it's caused us strife.

I wonder where it all began,
And if there ever was a plan.
If searched on Google would I find,
'Twas hit-or-miss, or well designed?

On June sixteenth nineteen-o-three,
Ford Motor launched the Model T.
Assembly lines meant mass produced:
Affordable, was introduced.

Soon everybody owned a T.
But where to park 'em; you tell me!
Town planners met and soon foretell.
Spots straight-in, slant, and parallel.

Now, light years past the horse and cart,
We know how parking got its start.
But still however, parking's sparse,
And sometimes progress seems a farce.

Thank goodness we have choices now,
Soon *no more parking* we'll avow.
We'll Uber if the price is right.
Take Lyft, if Uber's schedule's tight.

And if you just cannot decide,
There's one more choice you've not yet tried.
This always seems to save the day;
Just pull on in and go valet.

"The three major administrative problems on a campus are sex for the students, athletics for the alumni, and parking for the faculty."

Robert M. Hutchins

"You know, somebody actually complimented me on my driving today. They left a little note on the windscreen, it said Parking Fine."

Tommy Cooper

"When I get real bored, I like to drive downtown and get a great parking spot, then sit in my car and count how many people ask me if I'm leaving."

Stephen Wright

"Now that women are jockeys, baseball umpires, atomic scientists, and business executives, maybe someday they can master parallel parking."

Bill Vaughan

"When Solomon said there was a time and a place for everything he had not encountered the problem of parking his automobile."

Bob Edwards

"The way humans hunt for parking and the way animals hunt for food are not as different as you might think."

Tom Vanderbilt

36. "Sweet Dream"

Sometimes, it's hard to distinguish dreams from reality. The most memorable and vivid dreams occur during REM sleep, when the brain is most active. That's when it's sometimes difficult to discern while dreaming, whether one is awake or asleep.

This sleepyhead thought he was locked inside a Krispy Kreme donut store overnight. He had visited Krispy Kreme many times before and was totally enamored by the efficient workings of their elaborate donut making system. So in his dream, he was all alone and quite startled when he heard someone enter the store. So he hid while the night watchman made his rounds. When the watchman left the premises, our guy was finally able to try running the sophisticated system and make donuts all by himself. But was he really dreaming all this time, or was he actually there making donuts?

What a nightmare! No, sweet dream.
I'm locked inside a Krispy Kreme.
Startled, and in fact amazed,
I dreamt I ate two dozen glazed.

Time the watchman made his rounds,
I must have gained some fifteen pounds.
Glancing 'bout he said: *That's that!*
Then grabbed two crullers, and a hat.

Now outside the shop's front door,
I heard his lonely engine roar.
Soon he's swallowed by the night.
I'm focused now on what's in sight.

Clumps of freshly kneaded dough,
Begin a journey we all know.
Risen, fried, then flipped, and iced,
Our firm restraint then sacrificed.

All I want's to turn that knob,
And start my donut-making job.
Wavering, as in a spell,
I finally thought, oh what the hell.

Shuddering, it came alive.
Then somehow surged to overdrive.
Donuts flew both left and right,
And glaze spewed forth a sea of white.

Seems so real, so very real;
The glaze, the mess, and all I feel.
Should I run, or should I clean?
There's not a simple in-between.

Next, I yearned to be awake,
My donut dream I'd soon forsake.
Then, I heard my wife declare:
So, what's that white stuff in your hair?

"My husband and I went to Bald Head Island for our four-year anniversary. We spent the night in bed with champagne, tequila and Krispy Kreme doughnuts and watched a boxing match on Showtime."

Teri Polo

"Wait. Why am I thinking about Krispy Kreme's? We're supposed to be exercising."

Meg Cabot

"Now, have I ever been tempted to break into a Krispy Kreme doughnut store in the middle of the night? Oh, yeah. God help us if I had a minibar stocked with cheesecake and chicken-fried steak."

Mike Huckabee

"It's simple. Eat well, exercise and get lots of sleep but make sure you indulge occasionally. At my age, I think, what the hell, and eat a Krispy Kreme doughnut!"

Michelle Pfeiffer

37. "Where Did I Lose my Mind?"

The older I get, the more times I misplace things or lose them entirely. In talking with some of my senior colleagues, this seems to be a universal conundrum. Sometimes, I feel like I'm losing my mind. *Where Did I Lose My Mind* was chosen among many poems to be published by The Society of Classical Poets.

I just found my glasses on top of my head.
My iPhone had dropped to the floor from my bed.
The car keys I lost were much harder to find.
Oh, where in the world did this fool lose his mind?

My shades I just found neath the seat of my car.
The wallet I lost, I had left at a bar.
My Kindle passed over, as if I were blind.
Oh, where in the world did this fool lose his mind?

I found the remote in the sofa someplace.
Umbrellas I've lost without even a trace.
My pen has just vanished, with papers unsigned.
Oh, where in the world did this fool lose his mind?

My doctor, good doctor, what's happened to me?
I've lost my sane mind and so please hear my plea.
You've lived a long time sir, in this senior stage,
The only thing wrong is your elderly age.

"Got up this morning and could not find my glasses. Finally had to seek assistance.
Kate Winslet found them inside a flower arrangement."

Emma Thompson

"Of all the things I've lost, I miss my mind the most."

Mark Twain

38. "Hell-Bound"

In the book, *State of Affairs: Rethinking Infidelity*, by Esther Perel, she says that: *Since 1990, the rate of married women who report they've been unfaithful has increased by 40 percent, while the rate among men has remained the same. More women than ever are cheating,* she tells us, *or are willing to admit that they are cheating.*

It's distressing to read that cheating has become so prevalent in our society. While its true that overall, more husbands cheat than wives, the point that Esther Perel is making, is that wives are cheating in more and more numbers every year.

The woman in this poem cheats with very little deception and with no shame at all. Not that she flaunts her cheating in front of her husband, but she sure doesn't go too far out of her way to hide it. She enjoys cheating. She feels that she needs to cheat; perhaps for the personal validation and emotional intimacy she knows her marriage lacks. The deep, intense hurt caused by her blatant, scandalous cheating, is evidenced by her husband's final, permanent response to her unfaithful ways.

> With liquor on my lips,
> My panties in my purse,
> I tiptoed through our bedroom door;
> Things went from bad to worse.
>
> My husband, sound asleep,
> I headed for the bath.
> It wouldn't be the first time that
> I'd walked this well-known path.
>
> I heard his voice; I turned.
> He asked me where I'd been.
> The truth wanted to tell him all,
> But lies would always win.
>
> My lies that night were weak.
> It seemed I'm finally caught.
> I told him this, I told him that,
> But this is what I thought:

My men, they turn me on.
It's wrong, but I don't care.
And breaking all my wedding vows
I've never thought unfair.

His sad eyes said it all.
He'd yearned for love and lost.
And as he turned and walked away,
He cursed the lines I'd crossed.

What happened next was weird;
The realm of the bizarre.
He shot me in my cheating heart,
Then lit his best cigar.

And now, I'm just a ghost.
And in the clouds I dwell.
But I won't be here very long,
I'm on my way to hell.

"A mistake is an accident. Cheating and lying are not mistakes, they are intentional choices. Stop hiding behind the word mistake when you get caught!"

"I have learned that there are 3 major sins, To lie, to cheat, and to steal. If you are to lie, Lie to save a friend. If you are to cheat, Cheat death. And if you are to steal, Steal the heart of someone you love."

The Coach

"Shame on you for cheating on me, for reducing it to the word cheating. As if this were a card game, and you sneaked a look at my hand. Who came up with the term cheating, anyway? A cheater, I imagine. Someone who thought liar was too harsh, thought devastator was too emotional. The same person who thought, oops, he'd gotten caught with his hand in the cookie jar. This isn't about slipping yourself an extra twenty dollars of Monopoly money. You went and broke our lives. You are much worse than a cheater. You killed something, killed it when its back was turned."

David Levithan

39. "Never Stop Your Dreaming"

In my lifetime, I've had some really weird dreams. Periodically, I'll have discussions with my friends about our dreams. We wonder for instance, where do dreams come from? And, why are dreams so crazy? But no one seems to know any more than we do about those mysterious, nighttime thoughts.

Then one day last spring, I happened to notice that a small bunch of daffodils I had on my kitchen windowsill, had turned completely around in order to face the warmth and light of the sunshine outdoors. I turned them back around. Oddly, they soon turned around to face the sun again.

I thought, if the flowers know enough to turn to the warmth of the sun by themselves, it wouldn't be much of a stretch for me to think that they might have dreams as well. And if they actually did dream, what would they dream about.

That single thought unleashed a torrent of crazy ideas about all kinds of inanimate objects, emotions, and people, and what they might possibly dream about at night.

Boastful dreams of being humble.
Candles dream of being lit.
Cookies dream that they won't crumble.
Church pews dream that many sit.

Failure dreams of second chances.
Flooding dreams that rains will cease.
Lovers dream of great romances.
Wartime dreams of lasting peace.

Parents dream of kids achieving.
Worry dreams of faith and hope.
Preachers dream of flocks believing.
Hardship dreams that folks can cope.

Dreamers, never stop your dreaming,
One day soon they'll all come true.
Dreamers, never stop believing,
Dreams reward when you pursue.

"All our dreams can come true, if we have the courage to pursue them."

Walt Disney

"Hold fast to dreams, for if dreams die, life is a broken-winged bird that cannot fly."

Langston Hughes

"I believe in everything until it's disproved. So I believe in fairies, the myths, dragons. It all exists, even if it's in your mind. Who's to say that dreams and nightmares aren't as real as the here and now? You may say I'm a dreamer, but I'm not the only one. I hope someday you'll join us. And the world will live as one."

John Lennon

"Without leaps of imagination or dreaming, we lose the excitement of possibilities. Dreaming, after all is a form of planning."

Gloria Steinem

"Follow your dreams. I say to the young people, if you have a dream, chase it."

Karl Malone

"At the age of six I wanted to be a cook. At seven I wanted to be Napoleon. And my ambition has been growing steadily ever since."

Salvador Dali

"A dream doesn't become reality through magic; it takes sweat, determination, and hard work."

Colin Powell

40. "Last but not Least"

Well, this is the end of the line. I've finally written the last of the poems for my book. Now it's time for me to say thanks and bid farewell. So please enjoy this last tongue-in-cheek story. Please feel free to leave feedback. I'd like to hear from you.

The book's complete; my work is done.
I've had a blast; a lot of fun.
And now my book goes up to Jan
To fix mistakes the best she can.

She looks for flaws that I have missed,
Like punctuation—get the gist?
Then publishing is where it goes,
How long it stays there, no one knows.

But once they've printed scores and scores,
They'll ship 'em out to all the stores.
If all goes well, without a hitch,
I'll soon become quite filthy rich.

I think I'll buy a new Rolls-Royce.
I've thought this through, and that's my choice.
And then I'll buy a great big yacht,
And I'll pay cash right on the spot.

I'll go on book tours signing books,
To great big stores and tiny nooks.
And on TV, become a star;
The best known bard both near and far.

Then off to meet the President.
He's putting on a huge event.
And then I'll start my global tour,
And make a bunch of millions more.

If overstating my self-worth,
I'll need to come back down to earth.
But dreaming's fun, you must admit,
So why not dream the book's a hit?

"How lucky I am to have something that makes saying Goodbye so hard."

A.A. Milne (Winnie the Pooh)

"It's time to say goodbye, but I think goodbyes are sad and I'd much rather say hello. Hello to a new adventure."

Anonymous

"So long, farewell, auf wiedersehen, adieu adieu, adieu, to you and you and you."

Sound of Music

"I really don't want to say goodbye to any of you people."

Christa McAuliffe

"Saying goodbye doesn't mean anything. It's the time we spent together that matters, not how we left it."

Trey Parker

80Meh reen - *This is splendid. It did bring a huge smile to my face*

These are examples of the various accent, syllabic, and rhyming conventions I have used in my book. But there are many more variations from which you can choose.

A xXxxX 5	A XxXxXxXx 8	A xXxxXxxXxxX 11	A xXxxXxxXx 9
B xXxxX 5	B XxXxXxX 7	A xXxxXxxXxxX 11	A xXxxXxxXx 9
C xXxxX 5	A XxXxXxXx 8	B xXxxXxxXxxX 11	B xXxxX 5
B xXxxX 5	B XxXxXxX 7	B xXxxXxxXxxX 11	B xXxxX 5
			A xXxxXxxXx 9

A xXxxX 5	A XxXxXxXx 8	A xXxxXxxXxxX 11	A xXxxXxxXx 9
B xXxxX 5	B XxXxXxX 7	A xXxxXxxXxxX 11	A xXxxXxxXx 9
C xXxxX 5	A XxXxXxXx 8	B xXxxXxxXxxX 11	B xXxxX 5
B xXxxX 5	B XxXxXxX 7	B xXxxXxxXxxX 11	B xXxxX 5
			A xXxxXxxXx 9

A xXxxX 5	A XxXxXxXx 8	A xXxxXxxXxxX 11	A xXxxXxxXx 9
B xXxxX 5	B XxXxXxX 7	A xXxxXxxXxxX 11	A xXxxXxxXx 9
C xXxxX 5	A XxXxXxXx 8	B xXxxXxxXxxX 11	B xXxxX 5
B xXxxX 5	B XxXxXxX 7	B xXxxXxxXxxX 11	B xXxxX 5
			A xXxxXxxXx 9

The end words in lines "A" rhyme. I use true or exact rhymes. Some poets use near rhymes; rhymes that are close but not exact. Likewise, the end words in lines "B" rhyme. As do the end words in lines "C". The capital "X" designates accented syllables, whereas the small "x" syllables are non-accented. And lastly, the number at the end of the line represents the number of syllables in each line.

Once you have settled on a set of conventions, they are to be repeated in every stanza that follows. The closer you stick to the decided upon conventions, the better the poem. Some poets get lazy and sneak an extra syllable into a line, cheat a little on a rhyme, or settle on a multiple-syllable word with the wrong natural accents. Work harder, have patience, stick to it, and you will be writing technically perfect poetry.

Made in the USA
Coppell, TX
11 October 2022

84445668R00046